How to Draw Zentangle® Art

DRAWING ZENTANGLE® SEA LIFE

Hannah Geddes

Gareth Stevens PUBLISHING

Acknowledgments

The Zentangle® method was created by Rick Roberts and Maria Thomas.

"Zentangle"®, the Zentangle logo, "Anything is possible one stroke at a time", "Bijou", "Certified Zentangle Teacher"®, "CZT"®, "Zentangle Apprentice"®, and "Zentomology" are trademarks, service marks, or certification marks of Rick Roberts, Maria Thomas, and/or Zentangle Inc.

All the tangles in this book are Zentangle® originals created by Rick Roberts and Maria Thomas, apart from: Sand Swirl (page 11) by Karry Heun.

Please visit our website, www.garethstevens.com.
For a free color catalog of all our high-quality books,
call toll free 1-800-542-2595 or fax 1-877-542-2596.

CATALOGING-IN-PUBLICATION DATA

Names: Geddes, Hannah.
Title: Drawing Zentangle® sea life / Hannah Geddes.
Description: New York : Gareth Stevens Publishing, 2018. | Series: How to draw Zentangle® art | Includes index.
Identifiers: ISBN 9781538207215 (pbk.) | ISBN 9781538207192 (library bound) | ISBN 9781538207109 (6 pack)
Subjects: LCSH: Drawing--Technique--Juvenile literature. | Repetitive patterns (Decorative arts)--Juvenile literature.
Classification: LCC NC730.G43 2018 | DDC 741.201'9--dc23

Published in 2018 by
Gareth Stevens Publishing
111 East 14th Street, Suite 349
New York, NY 10003

Step-outs and Zentangle® Inspired Artworks by Hannah Geddes
Text by Catherine Ard
Outline illustrations by Katy Jackson
Designed by Trudi Webb and Emma Randall
Edited by Frances Evans

Printed in China

CPSIA compliance information: Batch CS17GS: For further information contact Gareth Stevens, New York, New York at 1-800-542-2595.

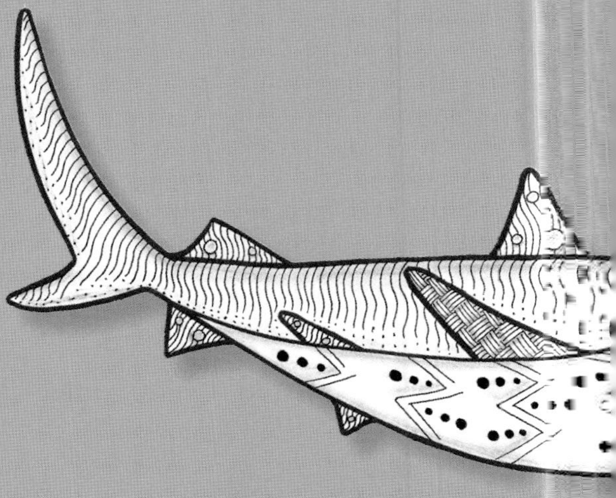

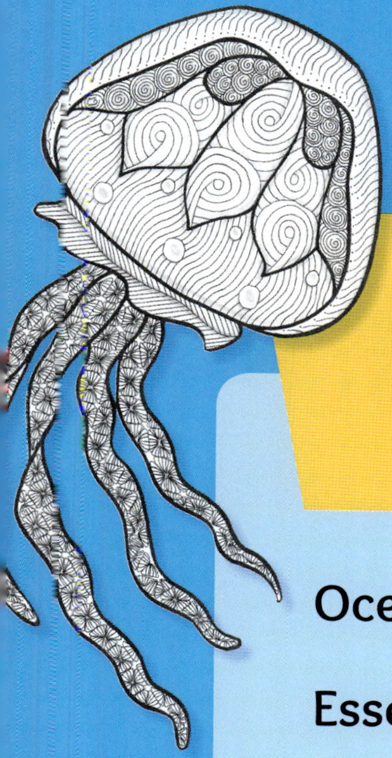

Contents

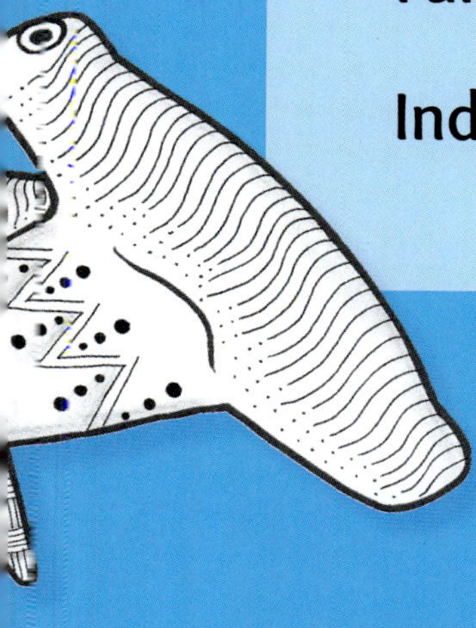

Ocean Inspiration

Zentangle® is a drawing method created by Rick Roberts and Maria Thomas. It teaches you how to create beautiful pieces of art using simple **patterns** called tangles. Tangling is a really fun, relaxing way to get creative, and it brings out the artist in everyone. You can tangle wherever and whenever the mood takes you!

Beneath the ocean waves live many fascinating and beautiful creatures. This book will show you how to create Zentangle® Inspired Artworks ("ZIAs") based on some of these mysterious animals. Each project features tangles perfectly suited to the creature, whether it's a playful dolphin or a sleek shark.

Pens and Pencils

Pencils are good for drawing "strings"(page 18) and for adding shade to your tangles. A 01 (0.25-mm) black pen is good for fine lines. Use a 05 (0.45-mm) or 08 (0.50-mm) pen to fill in bigger areas. You can use paints to brighten up your art, too!

Paper

Tangles are usually drawn on a square 3.5-inch (9 cm) tile made of thin cardboard. You can use any kind of paper, but if you want to make your tangles really special, use good quality art paper. Have some tracing paper on hand so you can trace the images in this book to use as outlines for your Zentangle® Inspired Artworks.

Useful Techniques

There are some special techniques you might come across when you tangle. A "highlight" is a gap or blank space in the lines of your tangles. Highlights can make your tangles look shiny!

An "aura" is a line traced around the inside or outside of a shape. Use auras to add a sense of movement to your art.

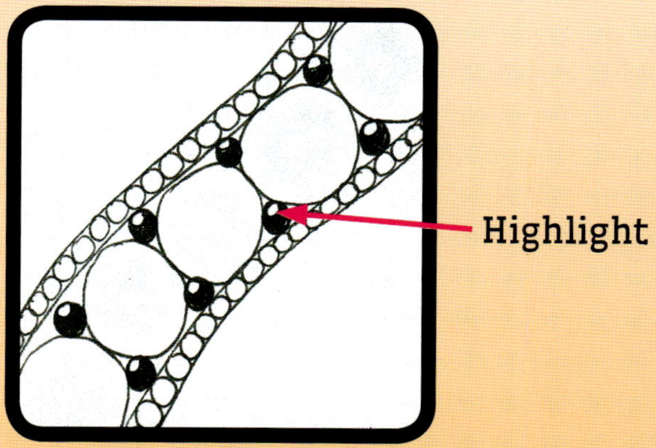

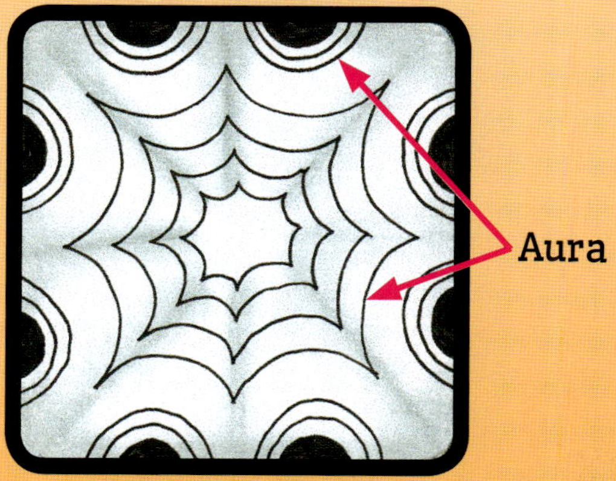

Essential Tangles

Here are some fantastic tangles to get you started! You can practice drawing each tangle on a square tile (see step 1 on page 18 for instructions). Each project in this book has a tangle key that tells you where to find the instructions for the tangles that have been used.

Tipple

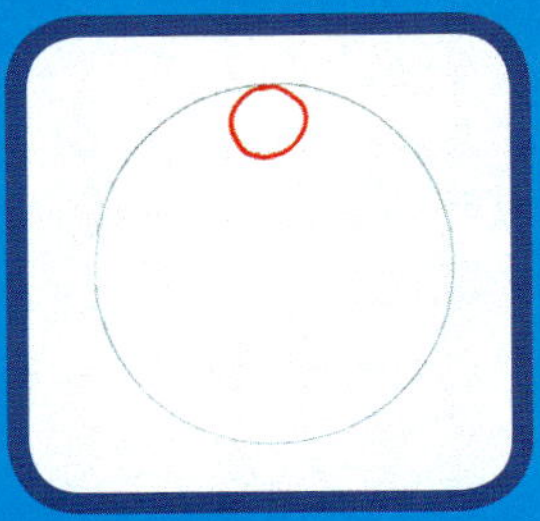

1. Start by drawing a small circle on your paper.

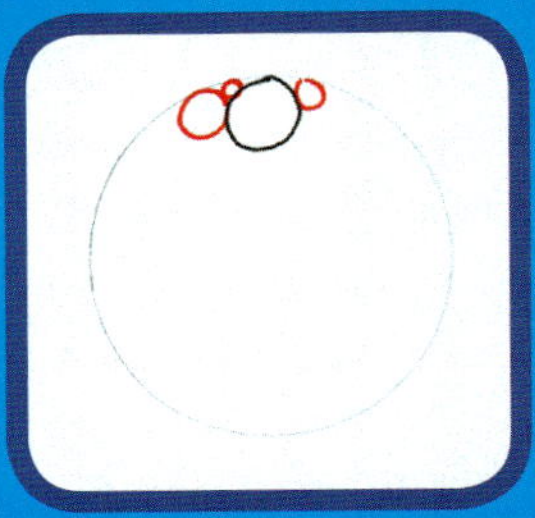

2. Add a few more circles around the first one. They can be any size you like.

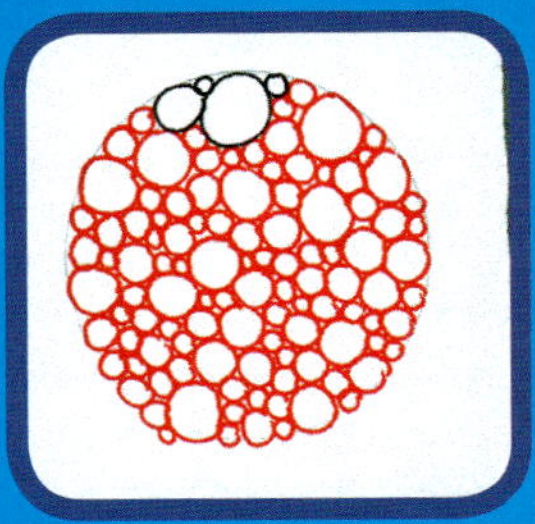

3. Keep drawing circles of different sizes until the chosen space is full.

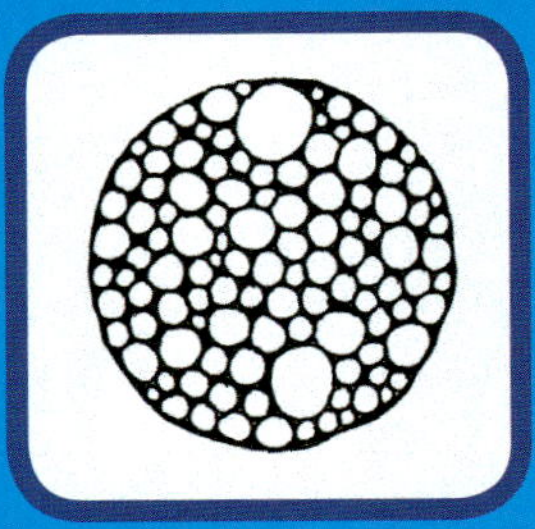

4. Shade in the spaces between the circles to finish your tangle.

Bales

1. Draw evenly-spaced **diagonal** lines across the paper.

2. Draw diagonal lines in the opposite direction to make a **grid**.

3. Draw bumps along the bottom of all of the lines you drew in step 1.

4. Then draw bumps along the top of these lines.

5. Repeat steps 3 and 4 on the diagonal lines that you drew in step 2.

6. Your pretty tangle is finished.

Keeko

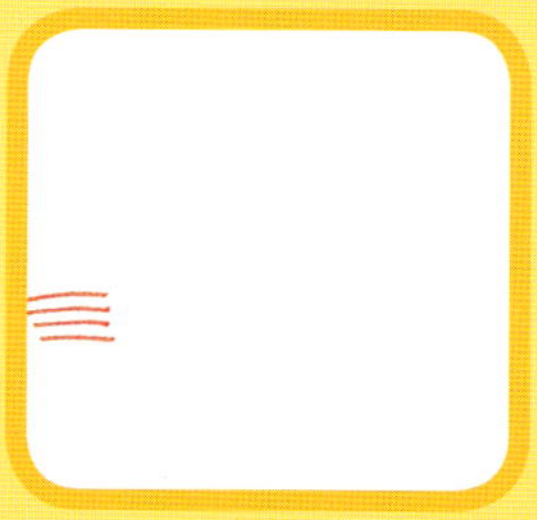

1. Draw four **horizontal** lines next to each other. They should be the same length and equally spaced apart.

2. Draw another four lines next to the first set, but this time make the lines **vertical**.

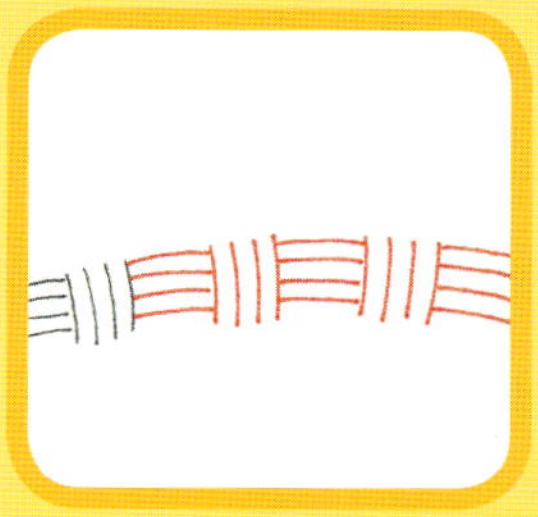

3. Repeat steps 1 and 2 until the row is complete.

4. Underneath each set of four horizontal lines, draw a set of four vertical lines.

5. Draw a set of four horizontal lines underneath each set of vertical lines.

6. Fill the chosen area, and then add some shading to finish it.

Cadent

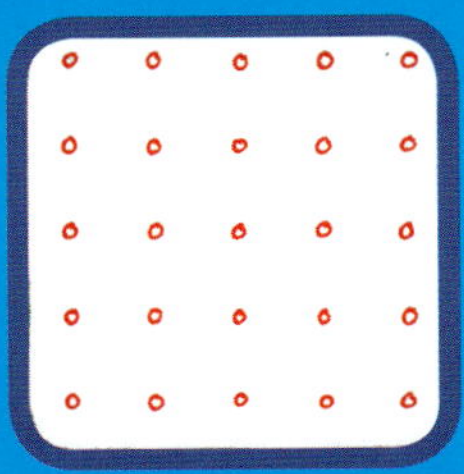
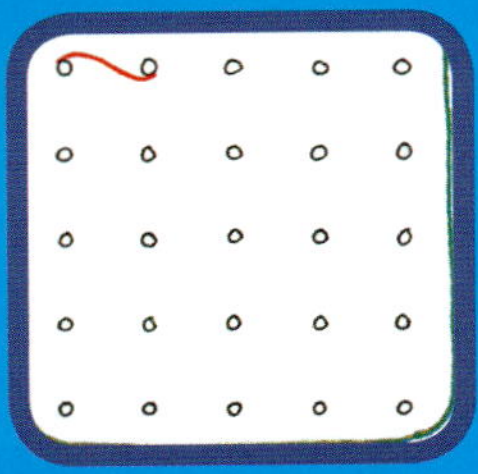
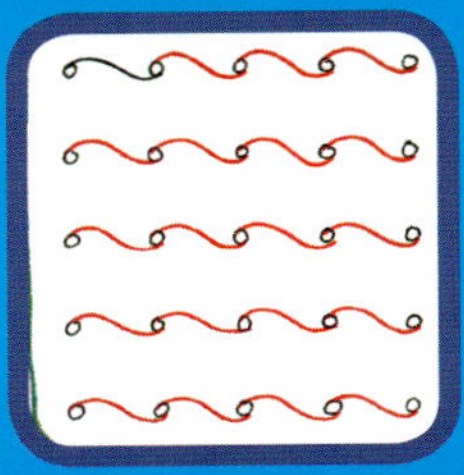
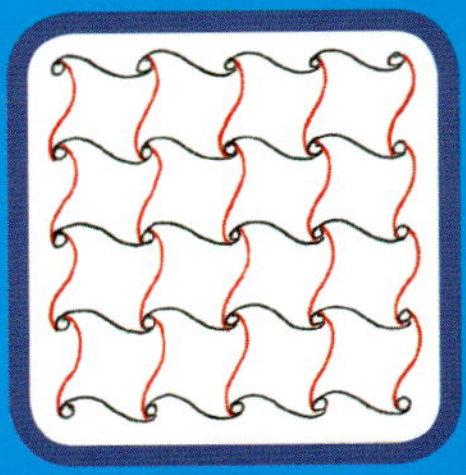
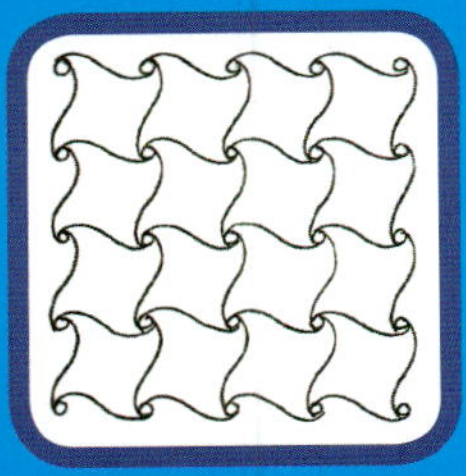

1. Draw a grid made up of small circles.
2. Draw a curve from the top of the first circle to the bottom of the second circle.
3. Repeat this pattern across each horizontal row of circles.
4. Now, use the same pattern to join up the vertical lines of circles.
5. Your Cadent tangle is complete.

'Nzeppel

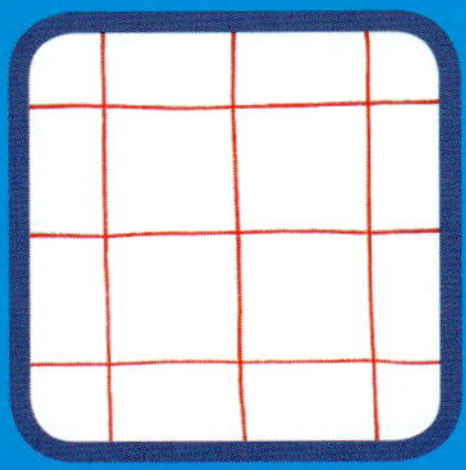
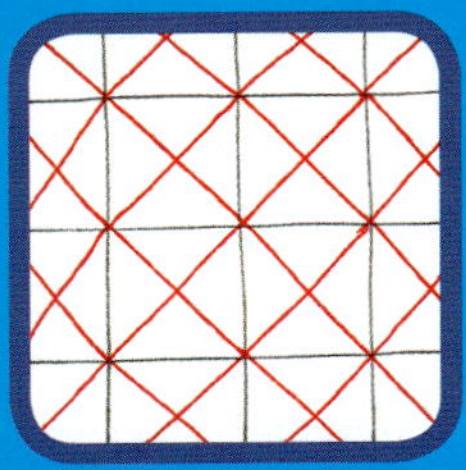

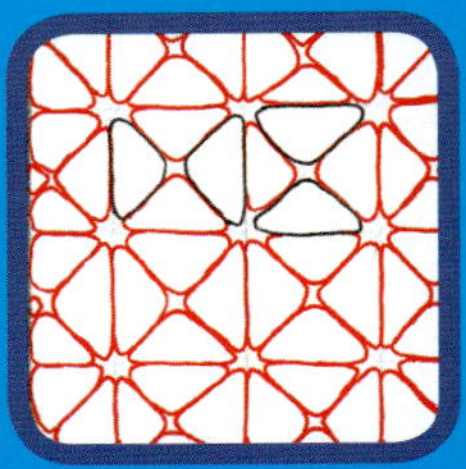
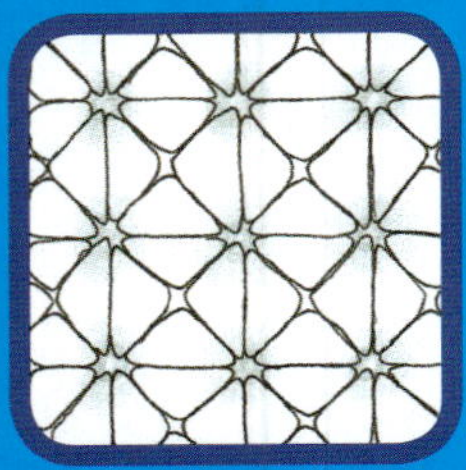

1. Draw horizontal and vertical lines over the paper to make a grid.
2. Now draw diagonal lines in both directions over the paper. They should be evenly spaced so they run through the middle of each square in the grid.
3. Each square in the grid should now be split into four triangular sections. Draw around the shape of each triangle, but round off the corners to create this pebble-like effect.
4. Continue to fill each square with triangles, as shown.
5. Add some shading to finish your tangle.

Printemps

This tangle is perfect for creating swirly textures.

1. Draw a dot in the middle of your page. Then begin to draw a small **spiral** starting from the dot.

2. Continue drawing your spiral. You can make it as small or as big as you like.

3. Once the spiral is the size that you want, turn the line in to close up the shape. You should have a smooth circle around the edge.

4. Add more spiral shapes around the first one.

5. Continue drawing Printemps spirals until you have filled the space.

Nipa

This wavy tangle looks like ripples and rising bubbles. It's perfect for any underwater picture!

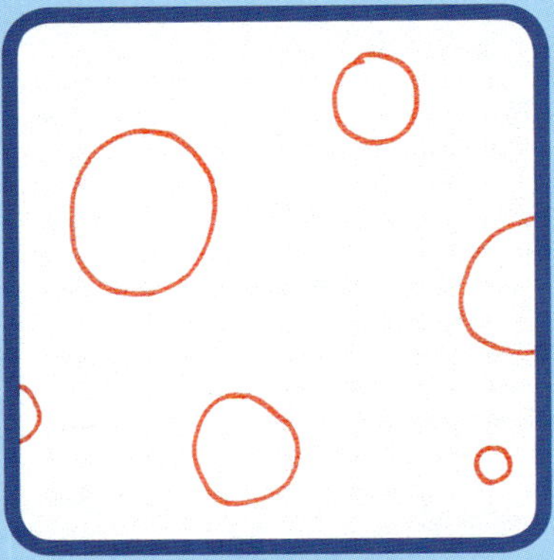

1. Start by drawing some well-spaced, different-sized circles across the paper.

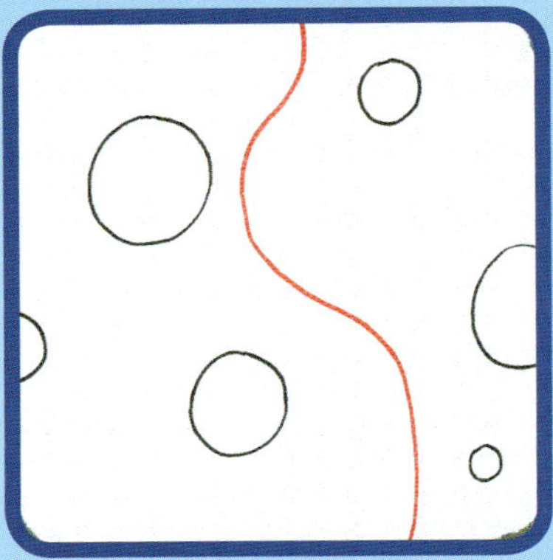

2. Draw a wavy line down the middle of the paper.

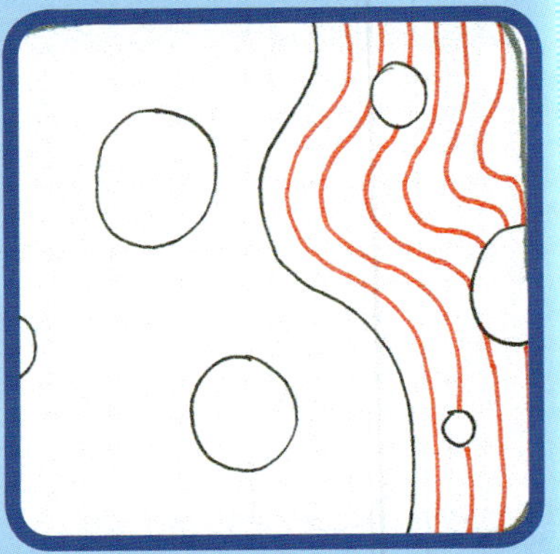

3. Draw more evenly-spaced, wavy lines on the right, following the shape of the first line. When you reach a circle, stop drawing and continue the line on the other side.

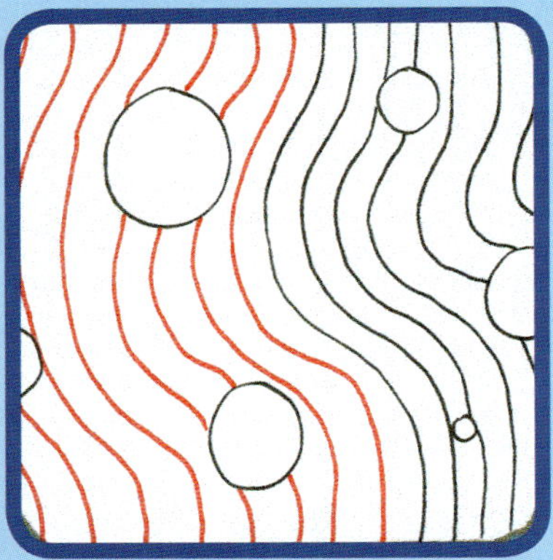

4. Now draw wavy lines on the left of the first line, remembering not to draw through the circles.

5. Add depth by shading inside and underneath each circle. Smudge your shading with your finger.

Tangle Tip!
You could fill in a few of the circles with your pen to vary the look of this tangle!

Sand Swirl

This swirly tangle of crashing waves will bring a sense of movement and energy to any marine animal.

1. Starting at the bottom of the paper, draw a slightly curved line with a circle at the end.

2. Draw another curved line, or aura, around the first line and circle. It should form a number 9.

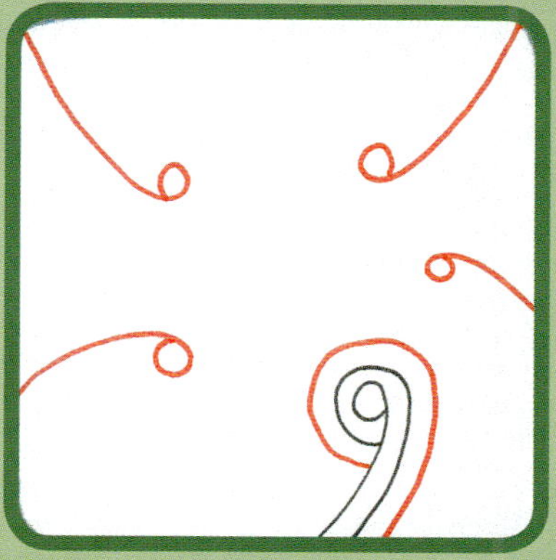

3. Add another aura to start to create a swirl. Then draw more curved lines with circles around the outside of the paper.

4. Continue adding auras to the first swirl until you have about five. Then add more auras to the other lines. When you meet another swirl, stop drawing and continue on the other side.

5. Finish with shading and smudging along the inside of each of the original curved lines.

Flukes

The overlapping diamonds in this tangle will make a striking set of scales for any fish!

1. Start by drawing diagonal lines across your paper.

2. Draw more diagonal lines in the opposite direction to form a grid of diamonds.

3. Draw a small diamond in the top of one of the diamonds and use your pen to fill it in. Then add three evenly spaced "Vs" below the little diamond to fill the shape.

4. Repeat this pattern in each diamond until they are all filled.

5. Your tangle is complete!

Flux

You can use this tangle to fill the bottom of your ocean with seaweed and pebbles!

1. Start by drawing a leaf shape. Decorate the shape by drawing a line from the bottom to the middle and adding a few dots above it.

2. Draw more leaf shapes around the first one, adding lines and dots inside them all.

3. Fill the space around the shapes with Tipple (page 6).

Tangle Tip!

Make your Flux shape tall so it looks like strands of seaweed swaying in the water.

Meer

This flowing tangle looks like ocean waves and strings of pearls.

1. Start by drawing two wavy bands with a space in the middle.

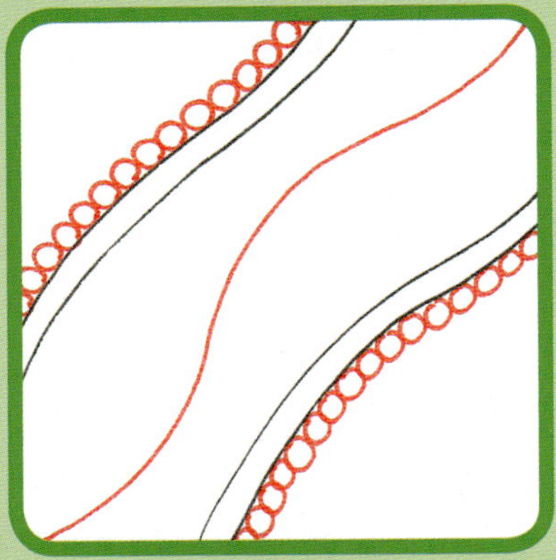

2. Draw a row of small, closely-packed circles along the outer lines. Draw a wavy line through the middle of the tangle.

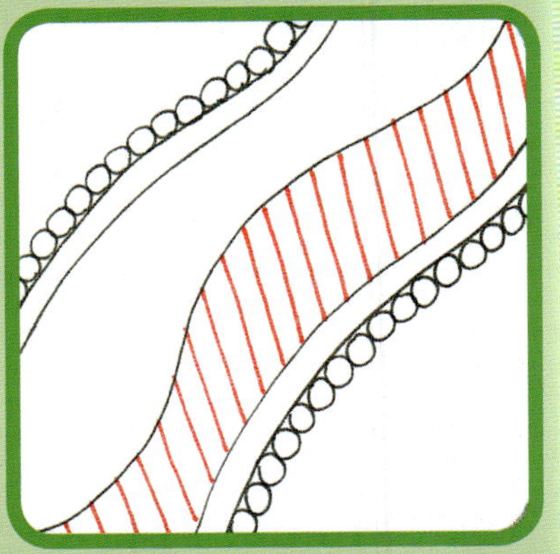

3. Fill the area on the right of the wavy line with evenly spaced diagonal lines.

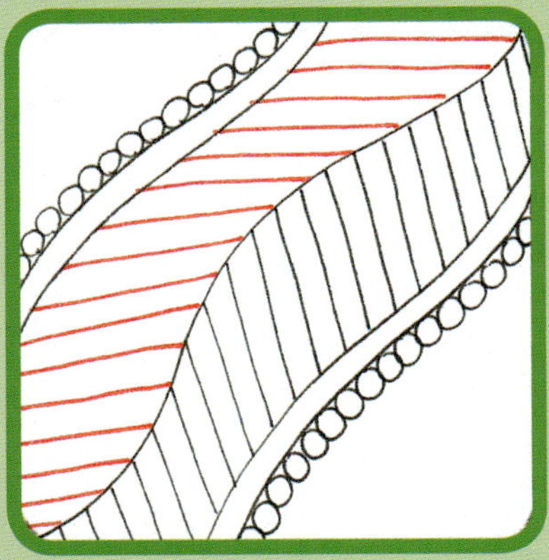

4. Now repeat on the other side of the wavy line with lines going in the opposite direction.

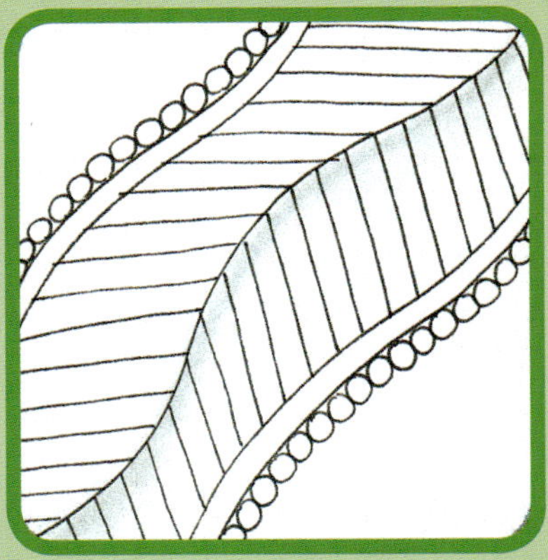

5. Add pencil shading below the wavy line and smudge with your finger to finish.

Msst

This delicate tangle is like threads of seaweed swaying in the water.

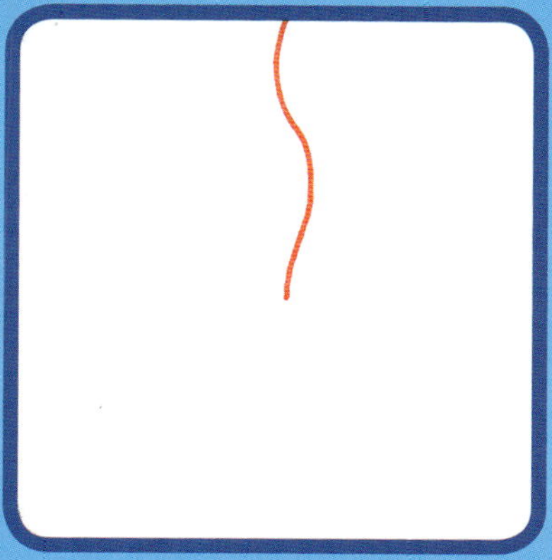

1. Start by drawing a wavy line at the top of your paper.

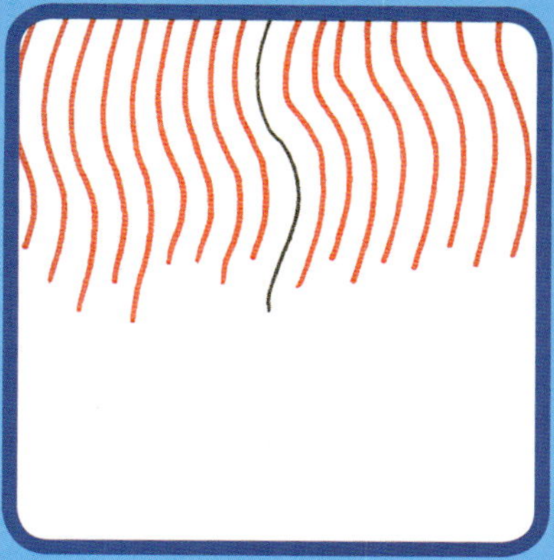

2. Draw evenly-spaced lines on either side of the first wavy line.

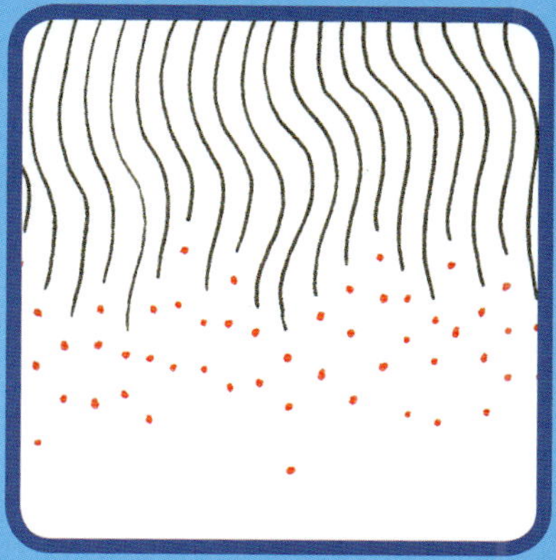

3. Add 3 or 4 dots below each wavy line.

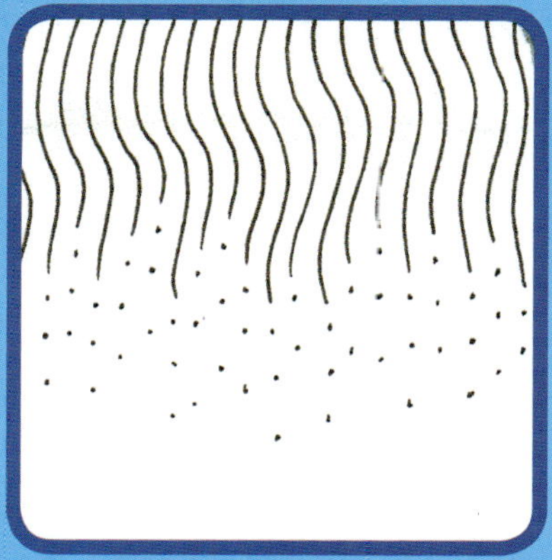

4. Shade and smudge across the middle of the wavy lines.

Tangle Tip!
Draw the dots at random below each wavy line to create a natural look.

Chartz

Give your pictures an extra edge with this spiky, spotty tangle.

1. Draw a diagonal zigzag across the page.

2. Draw a "V" shape inside each "V" of the zigzag, leaving a slight gap at the top.

3. Draw a small dot at the deepest point of the first "V" and fill it in with your pen. Add three more dots in a row, making each one slightly larger.

4. Now add rows of dots on the other side of the zigzag.

5. To finish, add some pencil shading on the right-hand side of each "V".

Tangle Tip!
This tangle would work really well for a shark picture. The zigzags are like razor-sharp teeth!

Festune

You could use this beach-inspired tangle to create clusters of barnacles, sea urchins, or tiny shells.

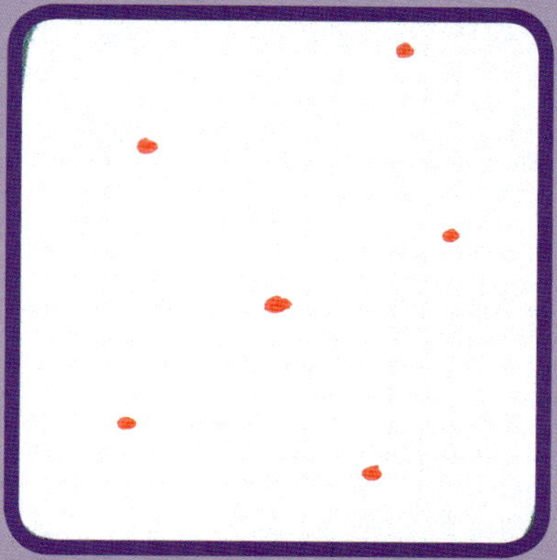

1. Start by drawing big dots across the paper.

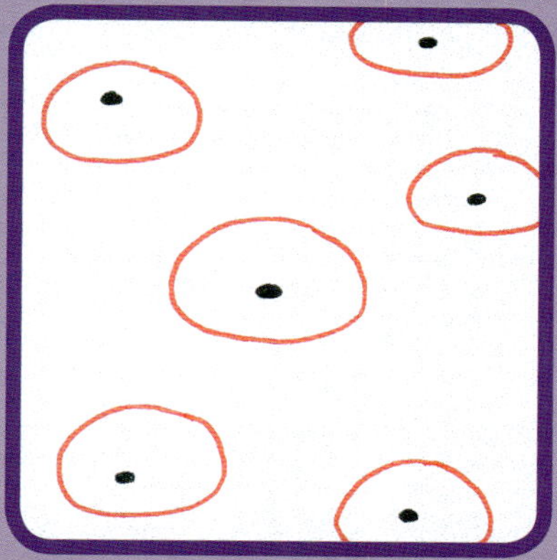

2. Draw a sideways oval around each dot.

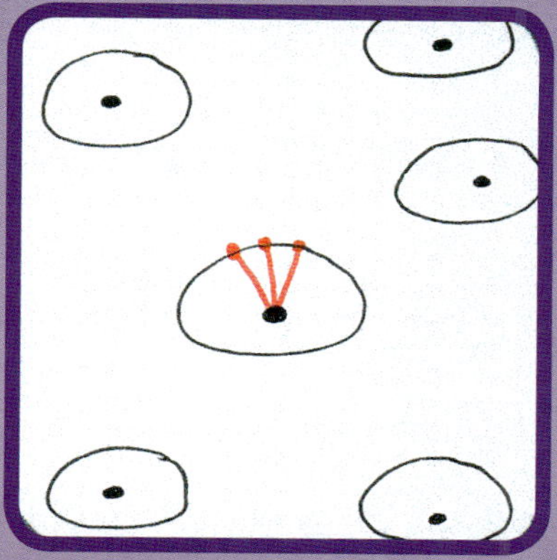

3. On one oval, draw a slightly curved line from the dot in the middle to the outside of the shape. Finish it with a dot. Repeat all the way around the oval.

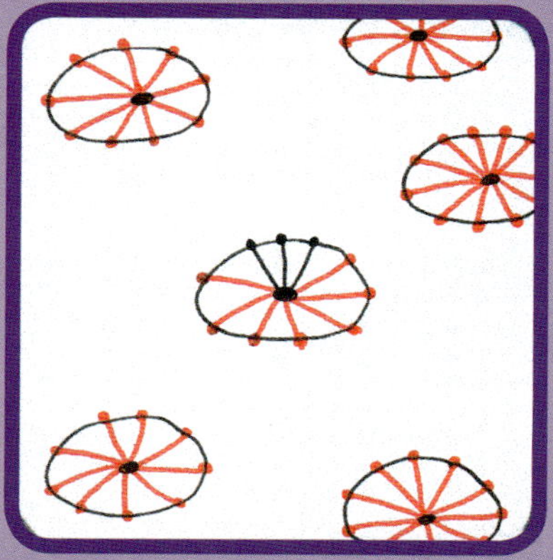

4. Continue until you have drawn lines on every oval. Draw as many lines as you like, making sure they are evenly spaced.

5. Fill the space with Festune for a busy look. Add pencil shading inside each oval shape to finish.

Strings, Tangles, and ZIAs

The Zentangle® method begins with drawing "strings." These are pencil lines that separate spaces inside a shape. The spaces are then filled with tangles to create your ZIA. Each project in this book starts with an outline of a sea creature with the strings already drawn in.

These steps show you how to build up a set of Zentangle® patterns on a Zentangle® tile. Tiles are good for practicing the tangles you've just learned. They can also be works of art themselves!

1. To create a square tile, use a ruler and pencil to draw four evenly-spaced dots for the corners. Connect the dots with straight lines.

2. Now divide the area using a string. Draw a dot in the center of the bottom line and strings from the top corners to the new dot. This will create three triangle shapes to fill.

3. Choose a section to fill and a tangle to start with. We've chosen Printemps (page 9). Starting in one corner and using a pen, carefully fill the area with the tangle.

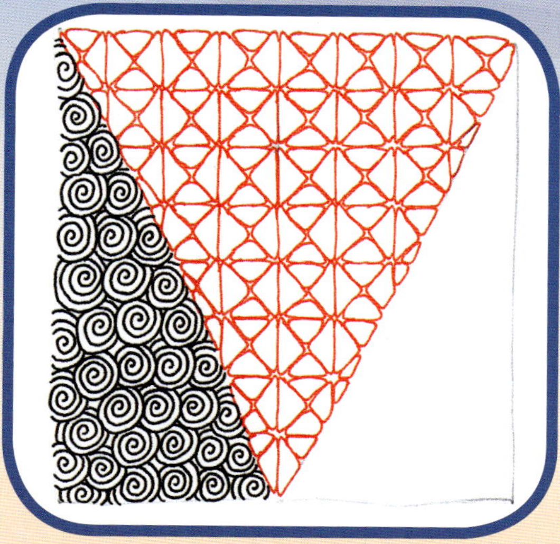

4. Now move to the next space created by the string. We've chosen to fill this section with 'Nzeppel (page 8).

5. In the final space, we've used Bales (page 7).

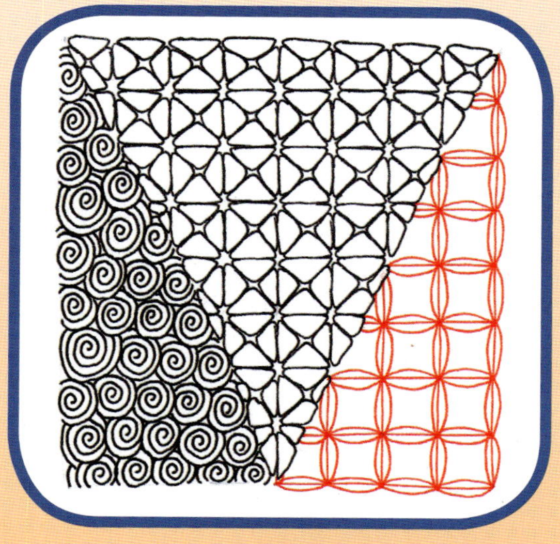

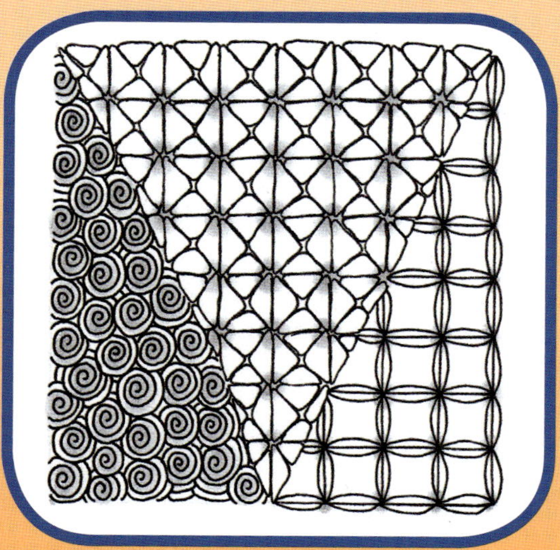

6. To complete the tangles, add shading to create shape and texture.

Now you're ready to start your own tangles!

Cute Seal

A seal's sleek body is perfectly designed for life in the water. Follow these steps to design a super swimmer of your own with some ocean-inspired tangles.

1. Draw or trace the outline of a seal with a string along its tummy. Add seaweed and the **seabed**.

2. We've used Sand Swirl for the seal's body, 'Nzeppel for its tail, and Keeko for its **flippers**.

3. We chose Meer for the seabed and Nipa for the seaweed.

TANGLE KEY

Festune: page 17
Keeko: page 7
Meer: page 14
Nipa: page 10
'Nzeppel: page 8
Sand Swirl: page 11
Tipple: page 6

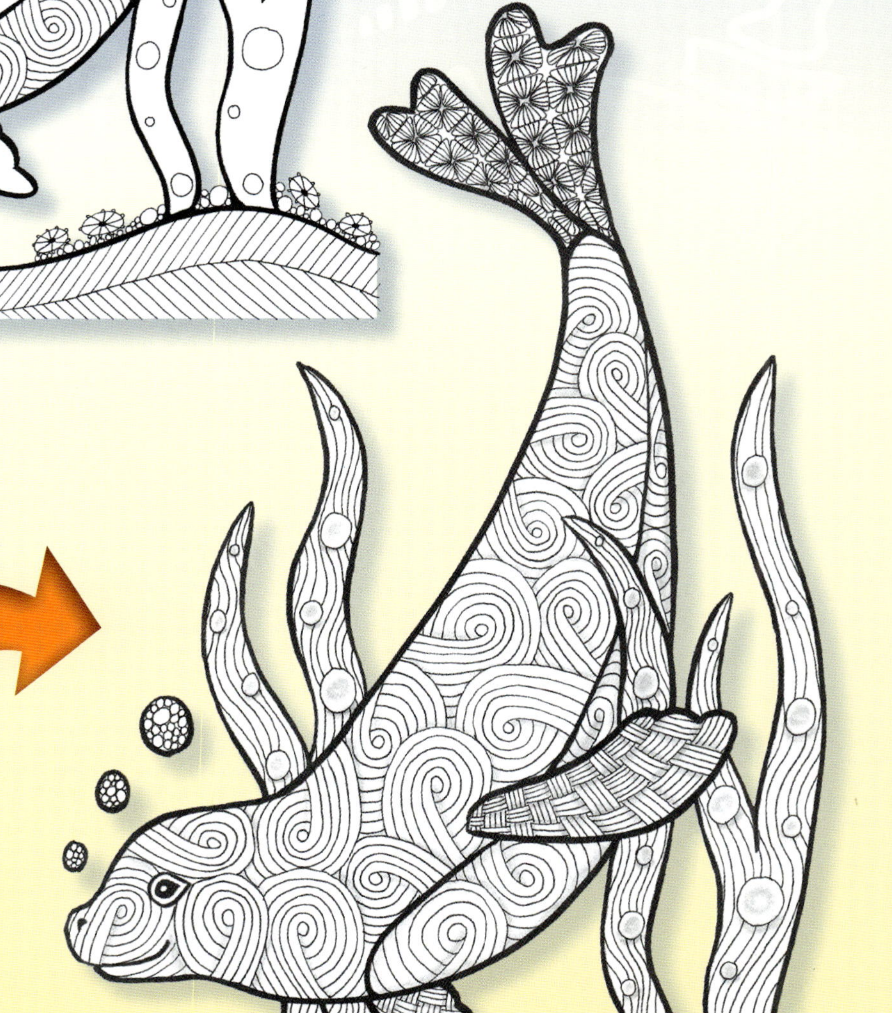

4. Finish the picture by filling the bubbles with Tipple and adding some tangles to the seabed. We've used Festune here.

Tropical Fish

Tropical seas teem with bright fish darting among the coral. Create a tang fish covered in ocean-themed tangles and eye-catching scales.

1. Draw or trace this tang fish's striped body. Add some bubbles, too.

2. Start by choosing a tangle for the fish's body. We chose Flukes for a nice scaly look.

3. Add some more contrasting tangles. We used Flux for the fringes at the top and the bottom of the fish, and 'Nzeppel and Tipple for the fins.

TANGLE KEY

Flukes: page 12
Flux: page 13
Msst: page 15
Nipa: page 10
'Nzeppel: page 8
Tipple: page 6

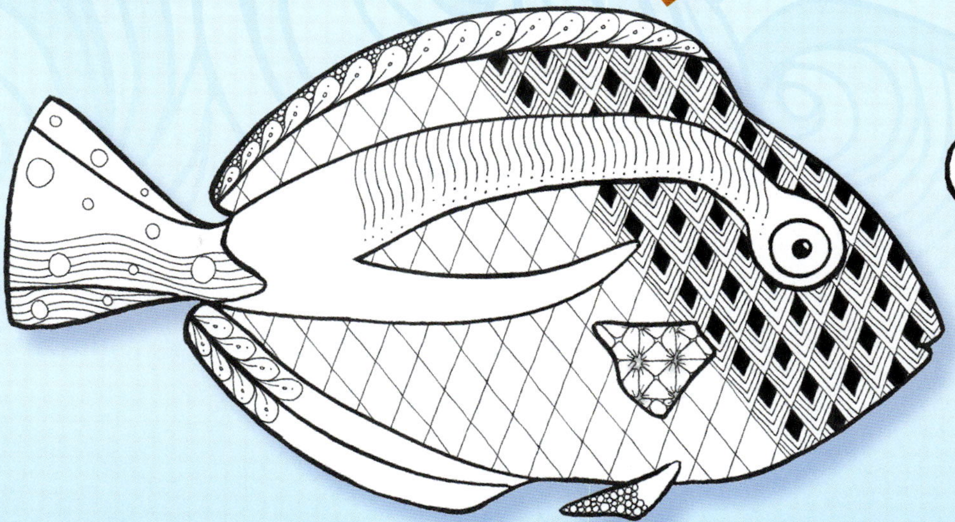

4. We tangled the tail with Nipa and the middle stripe with Msst. Shade and smudge along this stripe to give the fish a fuller shape.

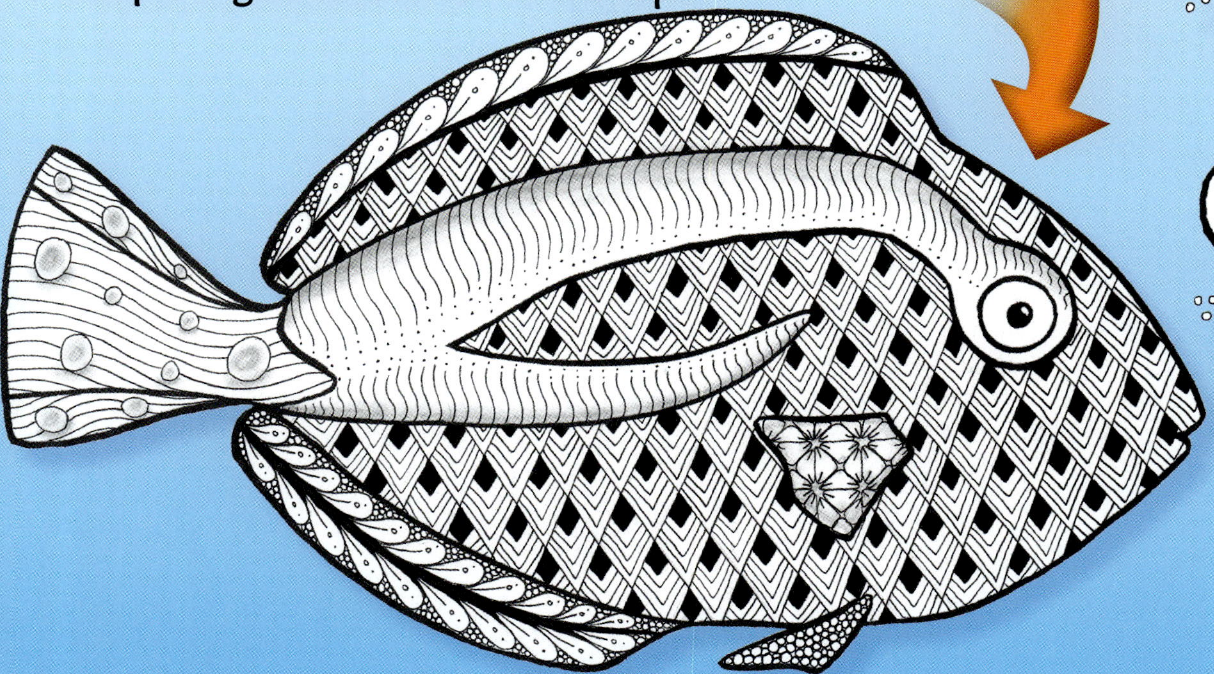

Playful Dolphins

Dolphins love to leap and splash as they speed through the water. Follow these steps to create a mother and baby dolphin with playful tangles to match their mood!

1. Draw or trace a mother and baby dolphin. Add a curvy string along each dolphin's back and an extra string on the mother's tummy.

2. Begin to add your tangles. We've used Nipa for the baby's back and Chartz for the mother's. The fins are filled with Tipple and the flippers are filled with Printemps.

3. We used Sand Swirl for the baby's tummy and Meer for the mother's. She has Cadent on her tail, too.

TANGLE KEY

Cadent: page 8
Chartz: page 16
Flux: page 13
Meer: page 14
Nipa: page 10
Printemps: page 9
Sand Swirl: page 11
Tipple: page 6

4. Give the scene an ocean feel with some strands of seaweed. A long, thin chain of Flux works well.

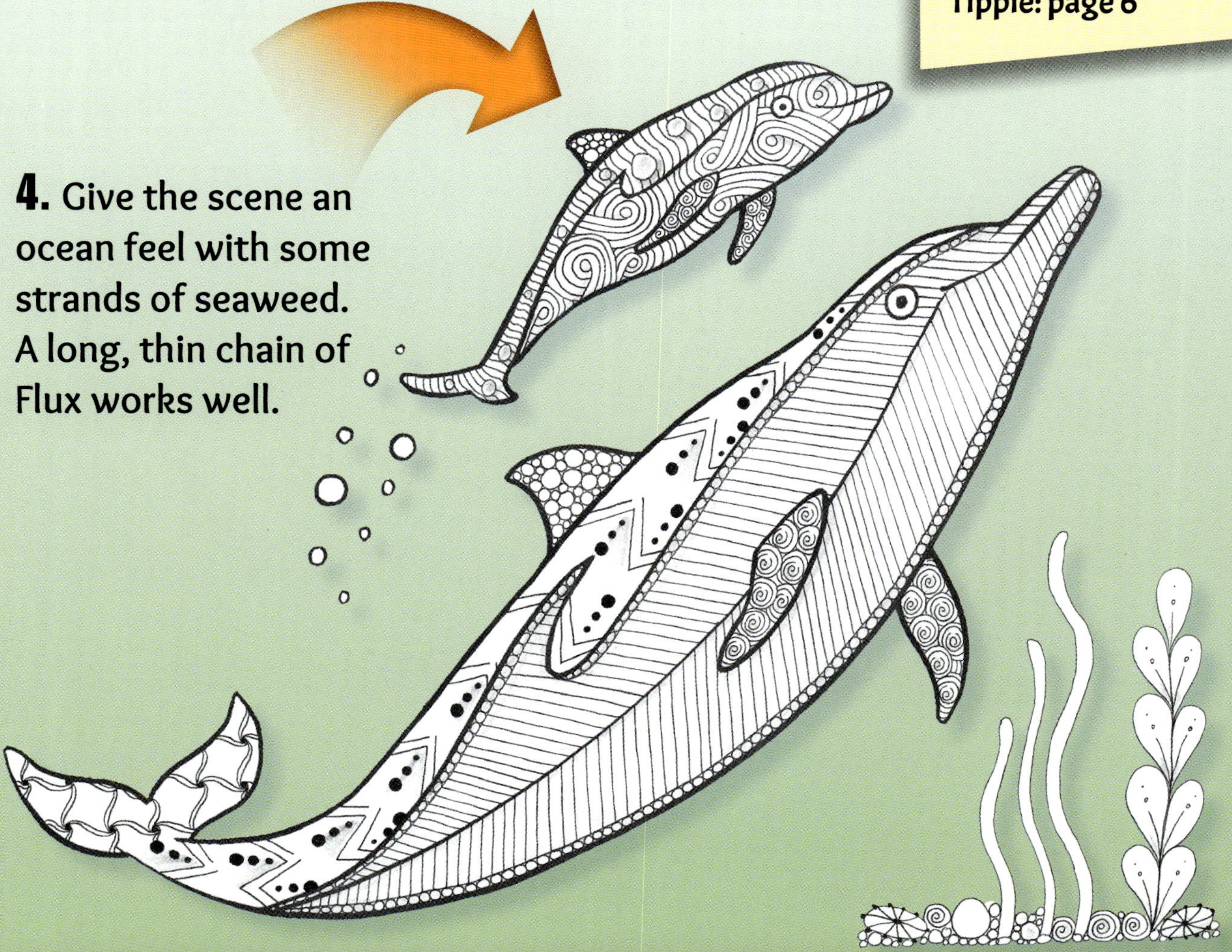

Wobbly Jellyfish

Jellyfish are not good swimmers, so they just drift along on the ocean **currents**. Tangle a wobbly jellyfish of your own with wonderful trailing **tentacles**.

1. Draw or trace a jellyfish with four wavy tentacles. Add lots of strings for different tangles.

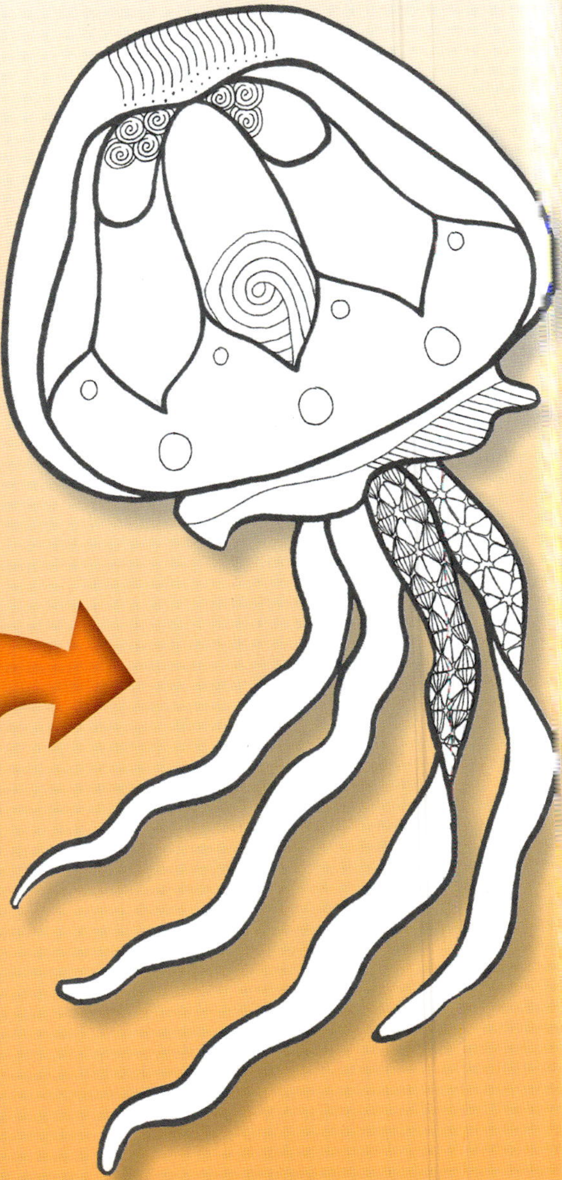

2. Start filling your jellyfish with tangles. We're using Msst for the top of the jellyfish's dome and Printemps for the four smallest inner sections.

3. The three large petal-shaped sections are filled with Sand Swirl and the bottom section inside the dome is filled with Nipa.

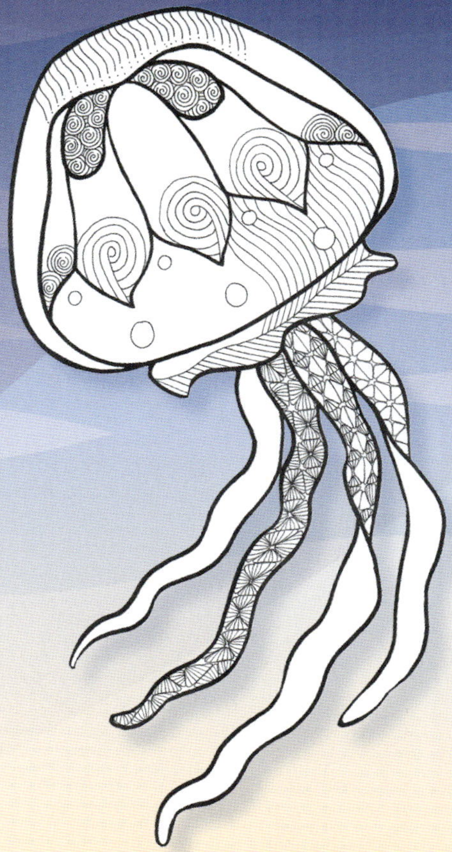

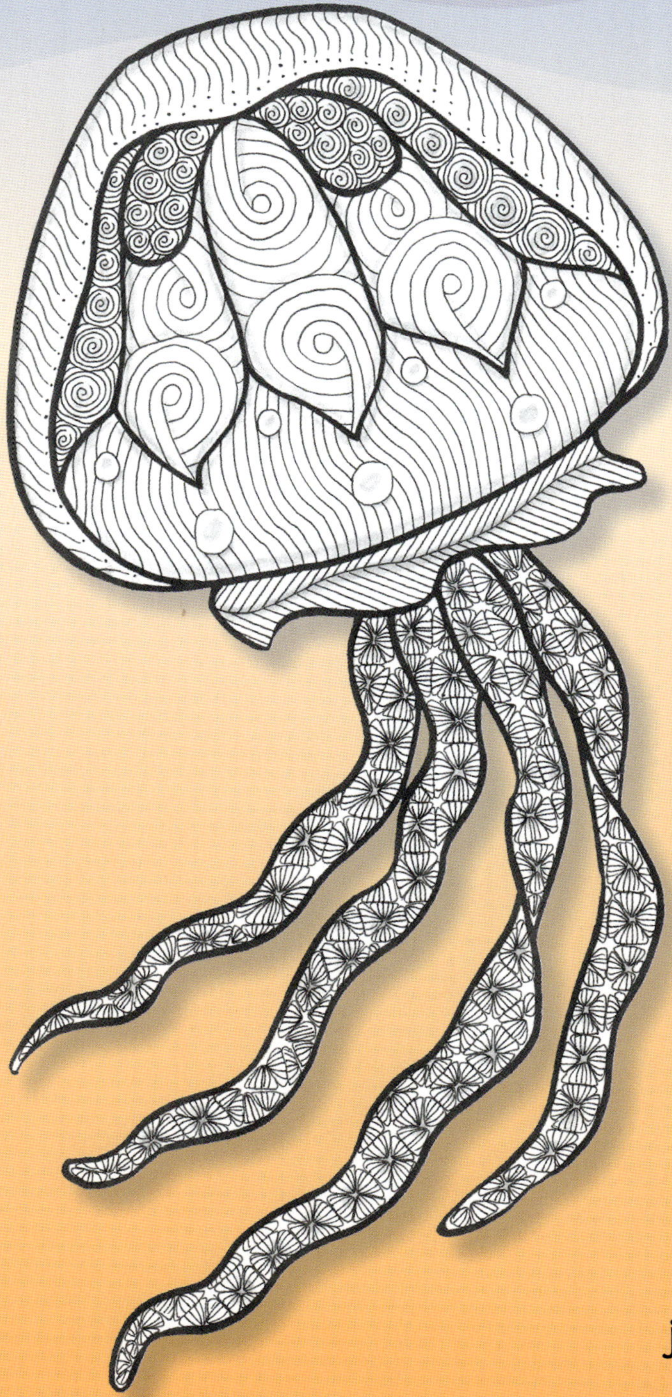

TANGLE KEY

Meer: page 14
Msst: page 15
Nipa: page 10
'Nzeppel: page 8
Printemps: page 9
Sand Swirl: page 11

4. We've used Meer without the circles for the frill at the bottom of the jellyfish's body and a twist on 'Nzeppel for the tentacles.

Hammerhead Shark

Hammerhead sharks sweep through the water, scanning the ocean with their wide-set eyes. Design your own deep-sea hunter covered with striking tangles.

1. Draw or trace a hammerhead shark with its wide head and long body.

2. Start to outline your tangles. We chose Chartz, with its zigzag pattern, for the shark's tummy.

3. The head and back of the shark are filled with Msst. We used Keeko for the front fins, and Nipa for the rest of the fins.

TANGLE KEY

Chartz: page 16
Keeko: page 7
Msst: page 15
Nipa: page 10

4. Add some pencil shading along the top of the shark's back to give its body a rounded shape.

Glossary

barnacle A small sea animal with a hard shell that attaches to a hard surface, such as a rock or the underside of a boat.

coral The skeletons of tiny sea animals found in tropical oceans. They can be many different shapes and colors.

current The movement of water in one direction.

diagonal A straight line at an angle.

flipper A wide, flat limb that is used for swimming.

grid A set of uniform squares made from straight lines or points.

horizontal A straight line that is parallel to the horizon, the imaginary line where the ground meets the sky.

jellyfish A water animal with a soft, bell-shaped body and many long tentacles.

marine To do with the sea, living in or near the sea.

pattern A set of shapes or a design that is repeated.

scales Thin, hard plates that protect the bodies of fish and reptiles, often overlapping.

sea urchin A small sea animal with a soft body and hard shell that is covered in long, thin spines.

seabed The ground under the sea.

seaweed A plant that grows under the sea or on rocks that are covered by the sea.

spiral A shape made from a line moving outwards in a circular pattern from a central point.

tentacle A long thin body part on some sea animals, they are used for feeling or holding things.

texture The look or feel of a surface.

vertical A straight line running from top to bottom, or bottom to top.

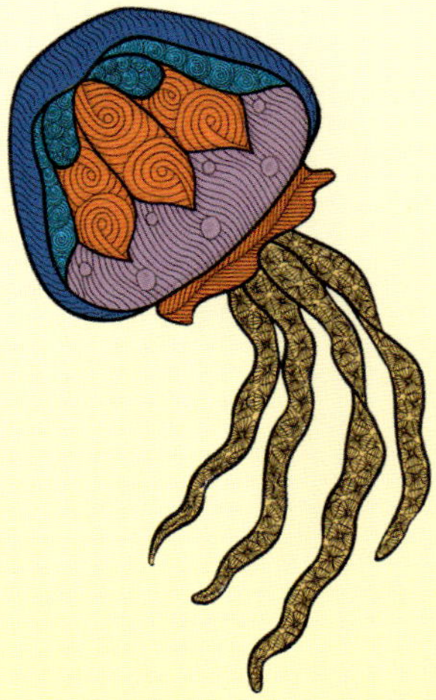

Further Information

Books to Read

How to Draw Dolphins and Other Sea Creatures
Peter Gray
PowerKids Press, 2014

Zentangle® for Kids
Jane Marbaix
Sterling Children's Books, 2015

Zentangle® for Kids: With Tangles, Templates, and Pages to Tangle On
Beate Winkler
Quarry Books, 2016

Websites

Learn lots of interesting facts about sea life and follow along with step-by-step drawing tutorials.
www.wedrawanimals.com/ocean-animals/

Check out this website for Zentangle® coloring pages and lots of other activity ideas.
www.kidsactivitiesblog.com/?s=zentangle

Head over to this website for lots of Zentangle® coloring pages, as well as other drawing tutorials.
www.supercoloring.com/coloring-pages/arts-culture/zentangle

Publisher's note to educators and parents: Our editors have carefully reviewed these websites to ensure that they are suitable for students. Many websites change frequently, however, and we cannot guarantee that a site's future contents will continue to meet our high standards of quality and educational value. Be advised that students should be closely supervised whenever they access the Internet.

Index